The Complete Oxford Travel Guide

The Essential Guide to Oxford's History, Culture, and Landmarks

By: Alexis Hartley

Introduction

Oxford, located in the picturesque county of Oxfordshire in England, is world-renowned for its prestigious university, rich history, and architectural beauty. Oxford attracts millions of visitors each year with its captivating blend of academic excellence, cultural heritage, and idyllic surroundings. We will delve into the essence of Oxford in this travel guide, providing you with useful information and insights to help you make the most of your visit.

Oxford's importance stems not only from its renowned university, which was founded in the 12th century, but also from its contributions to literature, science, and the arts. This city has inspired many writers, including J.R.R. Tolkien and Lewis Carroll, and its magnificent architecture has been immortalized in film and literature. Visiting Oxford is like entering a world of knowledge, history, and beauty.

When visiting a city as diverse as Oxford, a comprehensive travel guide is essential. It will help you find your way through the maze of colleges, libraries, museums, and other attractions that await you. It reveals cultural events, culinary delights, and hidden gems in the city. This guide aims to provide you with the tools to unlock the wonders of Oxford, whether you are an academic enthusiast, a history buff, a literature lover, or simply a curious traveller.

Prepare to embark on a journey through the hallowed halls of academia, stroll along charming streets, and immerse yourself in this enchanting city's cultural tapestry. Discover Oxford's secrets, uncover its stories, and make memories that will last a lifetime.

Getting to Know Oxford

Oxford, with its storied past and distinguished academic heritage, is a charming and intellectually vibrant city. Let's look at the key elements that define Oxford and make it such an appealing destination:

Historical Background

Oxford has a history dating back over a thousand years, with evidence of settlement dating back to Saxon times. The city rose to prominence in the 12th century, when the University of Oxford was founded, making it one of the world's oldest and most prestigious universities. Oxford has played an important role in shaping academia, politics, and culture over the centuries, leaving behind a rich tapestry of historical events and architectural marvels.

Cultural and Academic Relevance

The cultural and academic importance of Oxford cannot be overstated. The city's beating heart is the university, which is made up of numerous colleges. Its academic strength and intellectual heritage have drawn scholars, scientists, and thinkers from all over the world. The university's influence extends beyond education, with alumni making significant contributions to literature, science, politics, and the arts. The intellectual atmosphere that pervades Oxford inspires creativity, innovation, and critical thinking.

Famous Landmarks and Attractions

Oxford is brimming with iconic landmarks and attractions that reflect the city's rich history and architectural splendour. Among the notable highlights are:

1. Radcliffe Camera: A beautiful circular library that symbolises Oxford's academic excellence.

2. Christ Church College: One of Oxford's largest and most prestigious colleges, known for its magnificent Great Hall and links to Alice's Adventures in Wonderland.

3. Bodleian Library: One of Europe's oldest libraries, housing a large collection of books and manuscripts.

4. The Ashmolean Museum, the world's first university museum, houses a diverse collection of art and archaeological artifacts.

5. Oxford Botanic Garden: A tranquil oasis and the UK's oldest botanic garden, with an impressive plant collection.

6. Carfax Tower: A remnant of the 12th-century St. Martin's Church, this tower offers panoramic views of the city.

These are just a few of the many fascinating landmarks and attractions that await discovery in Oxford. Every street corner in the city reveals a different aspect of the city's historical and cultural heritage.

Prepare to be immersed in a world where academia, history, and culture intersect as you travel through Oxford. Admire the architectural splendour, interact with the intellectual atmosphere, and learn about the stories that have shaped this extraordinary city.

Planning Your Trip to Oxford

Careful planning is required to make the most of your visit to Oxford. Here are some things to think about for your trip:

Best Time to Visit

Oxford can be enjoyed year-round, but the best time to visit largely depends on your preferences. The city experiences a mild climate, with warm summers and cool winters. The spring and summer months (April to September) are popular, offering pleasant weather and the opportunity to explore outdoor attractions. Autumn (September to November) showcases the city's beautiful foliage, while winter (December to February) can be quieter and allows for a more intimate exploration of the city's indoor attractions.

Duration of Stay and Suggested Itineraries

The length of your stay in Oxford will be determined by your interests and the level of exploration desired. A minimum of two to three days is recommended to get a thorough understanding of the city. Here are some sample itineraries to get you started:

1. Classic Oxford Experience (2-3 days)
   - Day 1: Tour the historic centre, which includes the Radcliffe Camera, the Bodleian Library, and Christ Church College. Learn about Oxford's history and traditions by taking a guided walking tour.
   - Day 2: Explore other college campuses such as Magdalen College and Pembroke College, as well as the Ashmolean Museum and the Oxford Botanic Garden.
   - Day 3: Take a leisurely punt ride along the River Cherwell or Thames, visit the Pitt Rivers Museum, and

shop at the Covered Market for local fare and one-of-a-kind shops.

2. Literary and Cultural Exploration (3-4 days):
- Day 1: Go to the Weston Library to see the Tolkien exhibition, then explore the settings that inspired Lewis Carroll's Alice's Adventures in Wonderland and see a play or concert at the Oxford Playhouse or Sheldonian Theatre.
- Day 2: Expand your literary connections by visiting the exhibition rooms of the Bodleian Library and the Museum of Oxford, which showcases the city's history and cultural heritage.
- Day 3: Visit nearby literary sites such as Blenheim Palace, Winston Churchill's birthplace, or the village of Woodstock.
- Day 4: Indulge yourself in Oxford's vibrant cultural scene by attending a performance at the Oxford Playhouse or a concert at the Holywell Music Room.

Accommodation Options and Recommendations

Oxford has a variety of lodging options to suit a variety of budgets and preferences. The city has charming hotels, guesthouses, and boutique accommodations that are close to the city centre. Staying in or near the city centre provides easy access to attractions, restaurants, and public transportation.

Consider the following areas for accommodation:

- City Centre: Offers convenient access to landmarks, restaurants, and shopping areas.
- Jericho: A trendy bohemian neighbourhood known for its independent shops and eateries.
- Summertown: A leafy suburb with a more relaxed atmosphere and a variety of accommodation options.

Consider factors such as location, amenities, and previous guest reviews when selecting your lodging. It is best to book ahead of time, especially during peak seasons, to ensure your preferred choice.

You can ensure a well-organised and enjoyable trip to Oxford by considering the best time to visit, planning your itinerary based on your interests, and selecting appropriate accommodation. Prepare to be immersed in the city's intellectual and cultural heritage, to marvel at its architectural marvels, and to create lasting memories in this enthralling destination.

Exploring Oxford's Architectural Marvels

Oxford is an architectural treasure trove, with iconic university buildings, historic colleges, and cultural institutions. Here are a few highlights to look out for during your visit:

Iconic University Buildings and Colleges:
The stunning architecture of Oxford University contributes significantly to the city's allure. Many of its colleges are architectural works of art in and of themselves. Here are a few must-see college structures:

- Christ Church College: This sprawling college is home to the magnificent Christ Church Cathedral and Christopher Wren's iconic Tom Tower. The Great Hall, which appears in the Harry Potter films, is also impressive.

- Magdalen College: Magdalen College is known for its picturesque deer park and charming cloisters, as well as its stunning Gothic architecture. The tower of the college provides panoramic views of the city.

- Balliol College: Oxford's oldest college, Balliol features a mix of mediaeval and modern architecture. Its lovely chapel and grand hall are worth seeing.

The Bodleian Library and Radcliffe Camera: The Bodleian Library, one of Europe's oldest libraries, is an architectural marvel. Its structures range in style from mediaeval to modern. The Radcliffe Camera, a circular library that stands out as a symbol of academic excellence, should not be missed.

Christ Church College and Tom Tower: As previously stated, Christ Church College is an architectural marvel. It's Great Hall, which is reminiscent of Hogwarts, features intricate woodwork and a breathtaking hammerbeam ceiling. The Tom Tower, designed by Christopher Wren, is a prominent college landmark.

While not strictly architectural marvels, Oxford's cultural institutions are housed in impressive buildings that are worth admiring. The Ashmolean Museum, the world's first university museum, is designed in a neo-classical and modern style. Explore its diverse art and artifact collections spanning thousands of years.

The Sheldonian Theatre, an exquisite example of Christopher Wren's work, and the Museum of the History of Science, housed in the world's oldest surviving purpose-built museum building, are two other cultural institutions worth mentioning.

Take your time exploring Oxford's architectural wonders, taking in the intricate details, majestic facades, and historical significance of these structures. Each structure tells a story, linking the past to the present and highlighting the city's long history as a centre of academic excellence and architectural beauty.

Unveiling Oxford's Literary Heritage

Oxford's rich literary heritage inspires and fascinates book lovers and literary enthusiasts alike. Let's look at the city's ties to famous authors and literature, visit literary landmarks, and learn about the literary tours and bookstores that make Oxford a bibliophile's paradise:

Oxford's Communication and connection with Famous Authors and Literature: Oxford has long been associated with renowned authors, the works of whom have left an indelible mark on literature. Among the notable connections are:

- J.R.R. Tolkien: Oxford had a big influence on Tolkien's writing. He was a university professor who drew inspiration for his mythical realm of Middle-earth from the city's architecture and landscapes. Visit his grave at Wolvercote Cemetery, which includes a tombstone engraved with his pen names "Beren" and "Lthien."

- Lewis Carroll: The setting for Lewis Carroll's beloved Alice's Adventures in Wonderland was Oxford. Discover locations from Carroll's imaginative story by exploring Christ Church College and its surroundings, where he was a lecturer.

- Oscar Wilde: Oscar Wilde, the famous playwright and author, attended Magdalen College. Imagine the literary brilliance that once graced the halls of the college when you visit.

- Philip Pullman: Best known for his His Dark Materials trilogy, Pullman's books are set in an alternate Oxford, complete with recognizable landmarks and institutions. Explore the city from a new angle as you discover the links to his enthralling fantasy world.

Visiting Literary Landmarks

Indulge yourself in the literary world of Oxford by visiting the following landmarks associated with famous authors:

- Christ Church Meadow: Take a stroll through the picturesque meadow that inspired Lewis Carroll's Alice adventures.

- The Eagle and Child Pub: The Inklings, a literary group that included J.R.R. Tolkien and C.S. Lewis, gathered here. Sit where they used to sit and take in the literary atmosphere.

- The Story Museum: Immerse yourself in a world of storytelling and children's literature with interactive exhibits and installations that bring beloved stories to life.

To fully appreciate Oxford's literary heritage, consider taking a guided literary tour, which will provide insights into the city's literary connections as well as anecdotes about famous authors. These tours frequently visit historical sites such as the Bodleian Library, college campuses, and other literary landmarks.

Oxford also has a number of bookstores that cater to a wide range of literary tastes. Blackwell's Bookshop, one of the city's largest and oldest, offers a diverse selection of titles, including academic books and bestsellers. The Albion Beatnik Bookstore in Jericho is a hidden gem for poetry lovers and collectors of rare and used books.

You can deepen your understanding and appreciation of the rich literary legacy that pervades every corner of this captivating city by exploring Oxford's literary heritage, visiting literary landmarks, and immersing yourself in the city's literary tours and bookstores.

Discovering Oxford's Natural Beauty

While Oxford is well-known for its academic and architectural marvels, it is also endowed with natural beauty. Here are some ideas for exploring the parks, gardens, waterways, and surrounding countryside that highlight Oxford's natural beauty:

Parks and Gardens in the City:
Oxford has several parks and gardens where you can get away from the hustle and bustle of the city and reconnect with nature. Among the notable green spaces are:

- University Parks: University Parks is a picturesque parkland that spans 70 acres and is located along the River Cherwell. Enjoy leisurely walks, picnics, and peaceful river views.

- Botanic Garden: Founded in 1621, the Oxford Botanic Garden is Britain's oldest botanic garden. Discover its diverse plant collection, which includes medicinal herbs, alpine flowers, and tropical species.

- Christ Church Meadow: Adjacent to Christ Church College, this picturesque meadow offers tranquil paths for strolling and is an ideal spot to enjoy the natural beauty that inspired Lewis Carroll.

River Thames and Oxford's Waterways:
The River Thames runs through Oxford, adding to its allure and providing opportunities for water-based recreation. Consider the following scenarios:

- Punting: For a unique perspective of the city's landmarks and natural scenery, take a traditional punting trip along the River Cherwell or the River Isis (a section of the Thames).

- Thames Path: Take a stroll along the Thames Path, which provides scenic views and connects Oxford to nearby towns. Take a stroll along the riverbank and take in the tranquil beauty of the waterway.

Nearby Countryside and Hiking Trails:
Oxford is surrounded by beautiful countryside, making it ideal for outdoor adventures and scenic hikes. Consider the following alternatives:

- Port Meadow: Port Meadow, located just north of the city centre, is a vast expanse of open grassland that runs alongside the River Thames. It's ideal for peaceful walks and admiring nature's beauty.

- Shotover Country Park: Located just east of the city, this 289-acre park features woodlands, grassy slopes, and panoramic views of Oxford. Wander through the park's walking and cycling trails.

- The Oxfordshire Cotswolds: Explore the charming villages and rolling hills of the Oxfordshire Cotswolds, which are located a little further from the city. Take scenic walks and immerse yourself in the picturesque countryside.

Oxford's natural beauty will captivate you whether you choose to explore the city's parks and gardens, take a serene punt along the waterways, or venture into the nearby countryside for hiking adventures. These activities provide a welcome diversion from the city's historic charm, allowing you to appreciate the harmonious blend of urban and natural landscapes that makes Oxford truly enchanting.

Experiencing Oxford's Cultural Scene

Oxford's cultural scene is vibrant and diverse, with a wide range of artistic, culinary, and entertainment options. Here are a few highlights to help you immerse yourself in Oxford's diverse cultural offerings:

Theatres, Music Venues, and Art Galleries

Oxford has a vibrant arts scene that includes theatres, music venues, and art galleries that host a variety of performances and exhibitions. Among the notable establishments are:

- Oxford Playhouse: This renowned theatre offers a diverse lineup of plays, musicals, and comedy shows featuring both local and international talent.

- Sheldonian Theatre: The Sheldonian Theatre, designed by Christopher Wren, hosts concerts, lectures, and ceremonial events. Its magnificent architecture serves as a grand backdrop for cultural experiences.

- Modern Art Oxford: As a leading contemporary art gallery, Modern Art Oxford exhibits works by both established and emerging artists, creating a vibrant environment for artistic exploration.

Oxford hosts a variety of festivals and events throughout the year that celebrate various aspects of art, culture, and heritage. Among the most notable are:

- Oxford Literary Festival: The Oxford Literary Festival, which takes place every year, brings together acclaimed authors, poets, and speakers for engaging talks, panel discussions, and literary events.

- Oxford May Music Festival: This classical music festival showcases the beauty of classical compositions through performances by renowned musicians and ensembles in stunning venues throughout the city.

- Cowley Road Carnival: A vibrant street festival celebrating Oxford's diverse communities, the Cowley Road Carnival features colourful parades, live music, dance performances, and delicious international food stalls.

Food and Dining Options, Including Traditional English Pubs: Oxford has a diverse dining scene, with everything from traditional English pubs to fine dining establishments. Here are some suggestions:

- The Covered Market: Discover a variety of food stalls, delis, and local produce at the bustling Covered Market, which dates back to the 18th century. Indulge in the culinary delights of Oxford, such as artisanal cheeses, baked goods, and international cuisines.

- Traditional English Pubs: Discover the charm of the city's traditional English pubs. These establishments not only serve a variety of beverages but also traditional pub fare, allowing you to experience the flavours of British cuisine.

- The Jericho Café: Located in the vibrant Jericho neighbourhood, this café has a cozy atmosphere and a menu with locally sourced ingredients, making it ideal for a relaxed brunch or afternoon tea.

Oxford's cultural scene is sure to captivate you, whether you're enjoying a theatrical performance, exploring contemporary art galleries, taking part in vibrant festivals, or savouring culinary delights in traditional pubs or modern eateries. Immerse yourself in the vibrant tapestry of cultural experiences that Oxford has to offer by embracing the city's artistic and gastronomic offerings.

Day Trips and Excursions from Oxford

While Oxford has a lot to offer, there are several nearby towns, historic sites, and countryside destinations that make for great day trips and excursions. Here are some suggestions for sightseeing in the surrounding area:

Nearby Towns and Villages

1. Stratford-upon-Avon: Known for its Tudor-style buildings, the Royal Shakespeare Theatre, and picturesque riverside walks, this charming town is the birthplace of William Shakespeare.

2. Woodstock: The stunning Blenheim Palace, a UNESCO World Heritage site and Sir Winston Churchill's birthplace. Discover the palace's grand architecture and expansive gardens, as well as its historical significance.

3. Cotswold Villages: The Cotswolds region is famous for its traditional English villages

like Bourton-on-the-Water, Stow-on-the-Wold, and Burford. Take in the picturesque scenery, thatched cottages, and cozy tea rooms.

Historic Sites and Castles:
1. Windsor Castle: Windsor Castle, located just outside of London, is the world's oldest and largest inhabited castle. Explore the State Apartments, St. George's Chapel, and the lovely grounds.

2. Warwick Castle: A mediaeval castle in Warwickshire that features interactive exhibits, mediaeval reenactments, and spectacular views from its towers. Take a walk through history and learn about the castle's rich history.

3. Blaise Castle: This 18th-century mansion in Bristol offers beautiful parkland, woodland walks, and a unique folly castle. It's a wonderful place to explore nature and have a picnic.

Countryside Tours and Outdoor Activities:

1. Chiltern Hills: The Chiltern Hills, a designated Area of Outstanding Natural Beauty, offer scenic walking trails, charming villages, and panoramic views. Take a walk or ride your bike through this beautiful landscape.

2. Cotswold Wildlife Park and Gardens: This family-friendly attraction near Burford features a variety of animals and beautiful gardens. Explore the wildlife park and become immersed in the natural environment.

3. Bicester Village: If you enjoy shopping, Bicester Village is a luxury outlet shopping destination with a variety of designer stores and boutiques.

These are just a few of the many day trips and excursions available from Oxford. Exploring historic sites, involving yourself in natural beauty, or discovering charming towns and villages all provide a unique experience. Plan your trips around your interests to make the most of your time in the Oxford area.

Practical Information and Tips for Oxford

Transportation Options:

1. Walking: Because Oxford is a small city, many of its attractions are within walking distance of one another. Exploring the city on foot is a great way to soak up the atmosphere and discover hidden gems.

2. Cycling: Oxford is a bike-friendly city with numerous cycle paths and bike rental options. It's a convenient and environmentally friendly way to travel, especially over longer distances.

3. Public Transportation: Oxford Bus Company and Stagecoach operate a large bus network. Buses are a convenient mode of transportation for getting to places outside of the city centre.

Guidelines for Safety and Emergency Contacts

1. Safety Precautions: As with any city, basic safety precautions should be taken while in Oxford. Keep an eye on your belongings, especially in crowded areas, and avoid walking alone at night in secluded areas.

2. Emergency Contacts: Dial 999 for police, ambulance, or fire services in an emergency. Dial 101 to reach the local police in non-emergency situations.

Currency, Language, and Useful Data:

1. Currency: The British Pound (GBP) is the currency used in Oxford and throughout the United Kingdom. ATMs are widely available, and most businesses accept credit cards.

2. Language: English is the primary language spoken in Oxford. Because English is widely understood and spoken

throughout the city, communicating with locals is simple.

3. Hours of Operation: Most shops and attractions in Oxford have standard hours of operation, which are typically from 9:00 a.m. to 5:00 p.m. or 6:00 p.m. During peak tourist seasons, some attractions may have extended hours.

4. Wi-Fi and Connectivity: Free Wi-Fi is available in many Oxford cafes, restaurants, and public spaces. If you need internet access while travelling, consider purchasing a local SIM card or using a portable Wi-Fi device.

5. Visitor Information Centers: There are several visitor information centres in Oxford where you can get maps, brochures, and help planning your itinerary. 15-16 Broad Street is the address of the main visitor centre.

To help you navigate the city, it's always a good idea to have a map or a navigation app on hand. Don't be afraid to ask locals for directions or recommendations; they are often willing to help visitors.

Remember to check the most recent travel advisories and guidelines provided by relevant authorities before your trip to stay up to date on any specific safety precautions or entry requirements.

You can have a safe and enjoyable experience exploring the beautiful city of Oxford if you are prepared and informed.

Conclusion

Oxford has a rich history, culture, and intellectual legacy. Here's a rundown of its highlights, as well as some final pointers to make your trip to Oxford truly memorable:

Oxford's Highlights:
- Get yourself in the historic centre, with its iconic university buildings, such as Christ Church College and the Bodleian Library.
- Explore the city's architectural wonders, such as the Radcliffe Camera and the lovely college chapels.
- Explore Oxford's literary history by visiting sites associated with famous authors such as J.R.R. Tolkien and Lewis Carroll.
- Enjoy the city's cultural scene, which includes everything from museums and art galleries to theaters and live music venues.

- Take a stroll along the Thames or unwind in one of the city's parks or gardens.
- Consider taking a day trip to nearby towns like Stratford-upon-Avon or the picturesque Cotswold villages.

Final Recommendations and Tips

1. Plan your visit around your interests and allow enough time to explore the city's attractions. Oxford has a lot to offer, and it's worth spending time learning about its history and culture.

2. To make the most of your visit, consider purchasing a city pass or a guided tour. These can provide access to a variety of attractions as well as information from knowledgeable guides.

3. Check the hours of operation of the attractions and plan your itinerary accordingly. Some colleges and museums have set visiting hours, so it's best to plan ahead of time to avoid disappointment.

4. Take a walk through Oxford to fully appreciate its charm and discover hidden gems. Walking allows you to soak in the atmosphere and explore at your own pace because the city is pedestrian-friendly.

5. Sample the local cuisine and traditional pubs. While in Oxford, sample delicious food and beverages and enjoy a traditional pub experience.

6. Interact with the locals and solicit their advice. Oxford is a vibrant city with a friendly community, and residents are always eager to share their favorite spots and insights.

Keep in mind that some parts of the university's grounds and private areas may have restricted access. Maintain a respectful attitude toward the academic environment and be mindful of the city's residents.

You will have a truly unforgettable experience if you involve yourself in Oxford's history, culture, and natural beauty. Explore this amazing city and make lasting memories of your visit.

Made in United States
Troutdale, OR
08/02/2023